A DIALOGUE WITH GOD

TIMOTHY G. SAXE M.D.

To order additional copies of this book, contact:
Xlibris
844-714-8691
www.Xlibris.com
Orders@Xlibris.com

ISBN: Softcover   978-1-4134-7248-6
           EBook   978-1-6698-2575-3

Library of Congress Control Number: 2004097914

Print information available on the last page

Rev. date: 05/13/2022

A Dialogue with God,

is dedicated to the ones I love, those of you who know me and love me anyway,

and Cameron.

May my life always reflect the gentle love of God that exists in the world around us.

Ps 19:1-4

The heavens tell of the glory of God. The skies display his marvelous craftsmanship.

Day after day they continue to speak; night after night they make him known.

They speak without a sound or a word; their voice is silent in the skies;
Yet their message has gone out to all the earth, and their words to all the world.

The sun lives in the heavens where God placed it.

Introduction or Forward

The mere fact you seek God means you have already found him, for our God, the Great I Am that I Am, created the heavens and the earth. Just as with any great craftsman, their art being an extension of who they are, so too God can be found in all of creation if we would only look. This then becomes our life's journey, to walk with God experiencing His presence in our path of life as we experience his creation.

Where does one begin this journey? We begin in this moment, where we are now in the present, not searching the past or future. This moment is your path. Don't miss your path wallowing in the past or wandering aimlessly in the future.

St. John of The Cross in Spiritual Canticle (I, ii, 12), said "Seek Him in faith and love, without desiring to find satisfaction in aught, or to taste and understand more than that which is well for thee to know, for these two are the guides of the blind which will head thee, by a way that thou knowest not, to the hidden place of God. Faith.... is like the feet where with the soul journeys to God, and love is the guide that directs it..."

Building on the words of St. John, Thomas Merton said in his explanation of *"The Inner Experience"*, "Yet at the end of this journey of faith and love which bring us into the depths of our own being and releases us the mystical life culminates in an experience of the presence of God."

Renee Descartes, the father of deductive reasoning, stated that because he thought he therefore existed. He also reasoned that proof God existed is seen in the fact the world around him existed. If we search the world with faith and love, we too can find God.

I believe that we can see the proof of God's existence as well. We can touch God, feel God, and come to know God if we mindfully look at the world around us in all its splendor, glory and magnificence. We must realize this present moment is a true miracle. In mindful meditation, walking in the world, I began to see God's face in the smiling flower. I heard God's voice in the songs of the birds. In the fields and the forests, God has shown himself to me. I began to see God everywhere and in everything. There is no place I can go that I can escape God's love for me in this moment.

This love ignited a spark within the deepest parts of my soul so that my life now unfolds in a more mindful and spiritual way. I also began to record God's presence in my life just as one would take pictures of their growing children. When I see a leaf that has special color, a turtle, a lizard, or a bird, I allow that part of God to speak to me in love. The following pages are a record of my dialogue with God. God does not exist in the world as knowledge, but as love. As you seek God in your life you have already found him for that love surrounds you daily.

My prayer is that this record of my dialogue with God will set in motion the opening of your eyes, your ears, and your heart, so that in awareness and mindfulness of the present moment you may find your dialogue with God in the world around you.

1

To not observe God is to deny his existence. An object can not be known to exist apart from the observer. It is through the experience of the observer that an object finds its existence. The observed becomes part of the observer through experience. The object observed is however just our perception. Therefore, God cannot exist apart from the observer, the experience, and our perception. If there is only the eye that sees and nothing to gaze upon, there is no vision. If there is only a mind with nothing to be known, there is no knowledge. One cannot experience only the mind. The seer and seen must become one for there to be an experience. And yet, it is only the seen that is experienced. It is only the known that can be explored to gain knowledge. Likewise, if there is love with no beloved, there is only a vast void unfulfilled. The lover and the beloved must become as one. It is, however, only the beloved that is experienced and seems to exist, and the vast void becomes filled with the love that cannot be seen, touched, felt, but only known to exist in its perfectness. It is in experiencing this love, a love in which there is no fear, that we become one. God thus created man so that He could exist. It is therefore man's duty and obligation to observe God and love God. Our responsibility is to see and perceive God in all things that have been created by Him. We are God's life, and God's life is limitless. It has been said, "I in thee and thee in me". We have to observe not only our joys but our sufferings, our happiness as well as our fears. In doing so, we realize that our lives have no limits. We are the universe. The success and failure of the universe belongs to how we view our God. All around us life bursts forth with the miracles of God; a glass of water, a ray of sunshine, a bird, a flower, a raindrop. Reach out and touch the divine. In touching the divine, you find yourself to be at peace with all there is. The peace you find inside will ripple through the entire world and God will smile.

A person's perception … is their reality.
Bad news is only bad when we fail to learn from it… It is sometimes unwise to pray away the pain, for the
understanding and learning the pain brings is also prayed away...

The observed and the observer are one.

A glass can be either half empty, or half full… but it is still a glass … Life can be… what ever you make it !

Don't ask God for a bigger garden, ask to be able to tend the one you have been given. Be aware you are in your garden, are you ashamed of your nakedness? .. Your faith will clothe you and make you whole.

The paradox of Perception is that in being different, we are one. If the difference did not exist, there would be no perception. Thus in our perceiving oneness, we must assume difference does exist.

ETERNAL

Languishing in liquors,
Vapors of your love…
Sweetened by the stillness,
Pure as whitest dove.
Lily of the valley,
Your perfume fills the air —
A scent of love enduring
So subtle, but still there.

11

2

I was made to see God, because I was made in the image of God. The image that is for the world to witness. To say that the image of God is the reason for my existence, is to say that love is the reason for my existence, for God is love. The image of God is love, and so love becomes my true identity. My identity is not selfishness, pride or greed, but a love that brings peace, rest, fulfillment and joy. Therefore, there can be no judgment, only the image of God which is love. My only reason for being is to observe and be God's beloved. Empty words, booming voices over loud speakers, the clang of metal on metal serve only to provide a backdrop as the beautiful play of life is orchestrated before me. What I seek to find in the world is given to me. Therefore, I must choose wisely seeking peace and love as I look for God at every opportunity and find a world that blooms with warmth and compassion. God provides my every need, this allows me to look into the face of God and say, "I am truly loved, I am the beloved of God".

Nourish life with love. Don't starve life with fear. Attract life to you with love and compassion. Don't drive life away with fear and anger. Live life in this moment. Don't be dead in the past, or not yet born in the future.

Desire is the spark that ignites the flames of anger.

*When illusion is only the shadow of reality…and
the metaphor the distorted mirror of the illusion…
Reality becomes illusive.*

Wisdom is obscured by desire, just as Truth is obscured by illusion

Is the moth drawn to the Light by Love, or by fleeing from the... Fear of Darkness?

Some don't see the tree until they want to cut it down…
some fail to see life … till death.

3

The world is the manifestation of one being, our God. It flows forth from its source as a wave of love, streaming out for an eternity, in which time and space form no boundaries, in which the seen and the seer are one. This allows two aspects of reality to exist simultaneously, the unmanifested and the manifested, the seen and the unseen (2 Cor 4:16-20). Because we perceive the manifested, it is subject to illusion. Only in the unmanifested is there pure truth unobscured by the ego's search for reality. To see the pure truth of reality, one must see through the illusion of the manifested reality into the unmanifested. Therein lies the truth eternal, boundless and perfect. "Lord, increase my being that I may serve without fear. That I may see the seen without illusion. That I may know the known without judgment. That your perfect love may fill the vast void, and I may, in a unity of one being, become the perfect beloved, which I am, except for the illusion."

Love is a gift we should accept gladly

It is not that we need to learn more...rather that we must learn to forget
Our false boundaries

I Am who I am, because the turtle exists. The turtle is not the pond, and the pond is not the turtle. They only exist in relationship to each other, and thus are one. I am not the world, and the world is not me. But living in relationship, there is only ONE. We are separate from nothing, and bound by Love.

How wondrous is Nature, a beauty for all to see.
How precious are the mountains, every flower, every tree.
So we must not take for granted, lowly worm or honey bee,
for "What you did to the least of these you have done to Me."

You find yourself when you find GOD.
How you define God, tells one more about
you, than about GOD.

4

Our eyes are attached to our body, and thus to our physical being. They are also attached to the world, for they see the world and form a bridge with our being to the worldly. Our ears and other senses; taste, touch, smell, are only bridges to what is worldly. If we rely on them, it is difficult to transcend the world as did Christ. If we rely on our senses, it is difficult to perceive truth. We must therefore sense with our heart. We must look for love and compassion. For as God created the world, and all things in it, He did so with love and compassion. To feel this love and compassion is to remove the barriers that separate us from God. In removing the barriers, we find oneness with all that is. We find happiness, not diluted by our physical senses of what we "like and don't like". It is this perfect love that removes all fear. Fear then becomes the absence of love. By replacing absence with a flicker of love, no matter how small an amount, that love banishes fear. That love binds us and joins us to God, removing all barriers. Even the love in the size of a mustard seed, that love, small as it is, joins us with God.

This is what Jesus had in mind when he said that two must become one. For the mind cannot exist without an object to be known, and an object cannot exist without the mind. When the mind knows the object, the two become one. Only in their connectedness can they find perfection. Only when love has a beloved can it be fulfilled, and only when the beloved is loved does it find happiness. Only when the two become as one can one find perfection, moving from the manifested to the unmanifested, and in doing so catch a fleeting taste of the sweetness, a glimpse of perfect truth and reality, in which there is no illusion. There is only the "one being" that pours out all of His love to all that exists, His beloved. And when the two become one, there shall be heaven on earth. God sees Himself, God knows what He sees, and what He sees becomes the beloved that loves Him for what he is and what he has done, and the void is thus filled. We then are the seen, we then are the known, we then are the beloved. All that is asked of us is that we accept being seen, being known, and being loved. It is this gift that we should accept freely. In accepting it freely, the two become one, "in one being with the Father". In this perfect love, there can be no fear. There can be no birth. There can be no death. There can be no beginning. There can be no end. There is only "being."

Peace exists inside you, let it shine, and the world will be a more peaceful place for all.

Cast out all negativity
Set evil thoughts aside
Let go of your ego
Be not blinded by your pride
Begin to live your life
Not looking for the sin
But finding good in all God's gifts
A Peace that grows within.

Beside peaceful waters, I find my soul's repose…
in the silent voice of God… "I will put my spirit within you, and you shall live, and I will place you on your own soil"
God, as quoted by Ezekiel 37:14

A man can not tell where he is going... if all he sees is where he has been!

5

Before the world, darkness engulfed darkness, and God breathlessly breathed. Before the world, a thought emerged, and in that infinitesimal spark, darkness was conquered. The thought became a word, and the word became light, and in light things became seen, and breath became breath shared with the light and the seen, and the seen absorbed and reflected the light and the breath. The being then became expanded and the reflection grew and the word was illuminated creating all manifestations that they may be seen. God does not manifest in the world as knowledge but as love. Love is the word, it is the only word. It is the spark that conquers darkness and it originates from the *only* thought of God, for love is His only thought. Before the word and the thought, there was only engulfing darkness. Just as a sun's ray has no being without the sun, all manifestations of the world have no existence without the thought of God. This therefore answers the questions, "Why does the light shine, why does the mind think?" For these are the manifestations of the thought of God, and without these thoughts, darkness would engulf darkness and God would breathlessly breathe in an eternal slumber that knows not itself for there would be nothing to be seen. With nothing to be seen, there would be no seer and with no seer, nothing known. Void would be upon void, and yet we cannot fathom such emptiness. It is unthinkable, for there is thought, and through thought there is the word, there is seen and unseen, there is seer, the loved, and the beloved, and there is God. A God who in his glory and power transcends his glory and power sending forth His thoughts, becoming the seer and the seen, the loved and the beloved, being all things in one, indivisible and unchangeable. He is the universe. It is no wonder He called Himself**,** *I am that I am*.

I am not my fears, unless I allow my fears to become me
You may be unable to alter the present, but how you choose in the present alters the future.
Because you know what you are looking for does not mean you know the way.

If we learn from our trials
And each moment we devour
As manna sent from Heaven
Then evil has no power!
Evil only has the power we choose to give it

If you perceive God in all things, then it proves His existence…
But we are constrained in our "knowing" by the limitations of our minds and our perceptions…

6

It has been said that one must learn to love themselves before they can love another. This has been a root of religious psychology for over 3,000 years. The ancient mystics believed in an inner realization of the identity of the self and the one universal consciousness known to them as God or the Great Spirit. They believed that you could either strive to find God or strive to find the true inner self, and when you found one you found the other. Likewise, you may strive to find God manifested in the love that created the universe, or you may strive to find that love that exists within you. (As Christ said, "The kingdom of heaven is within you.") Either way, when you find that love, you find God and you find yourself. When you find God and self, you find the unity of perfect love. First, one sees themselves as a body, and as a body they are the servant. Next, they see themselves as a soul, and as a soul, they become part of God. But when they identify the self with the heaven that lies within, they have cast out all fear and all they are is Being, no past, no future, just present, the presence of God, perfect love.

This love does not begin with action, what we do, what we say, what we see, feel or hear. This love begins with a thought, an emotion deep within. That thought and that emotion leads to the words we say and the things we do, that are manifested by us and others as actions and beings of love. Where does the thought originate? Where does the feeling originate? If one searches the brain with all types of scans and technical instrumentation, they can find everything but the thinker of the thought. We have yet to be able to find God. Love originates from God and becomes manifest in our thoughts and emotions which we make into the worldly. As it was said in John, "In the beginning was the Word and the Word became flesh". Before the Word was the thought of God, and that thought was love. "For God so loved the world that he gave his only Son", and his Son was pure love. God continues this day to pour love into the world. It is for us to receive this thought and make it manifest. In doing so, we allow the Christ to be within us and shine through us so God's love can illuminate the world. We no longer react. We just love. Therefore, it does not matter what one does to us. Whether it is good or bad, harmful or joy producing. We just love. There is no action/reaction. There is just...*love*.

The best is yet to come,
When at night our dreams begin.
For the inner peace that you seek,
Begins when you search within.

The fruit of our labor is the manifestation of our love,
and thereby gives it value.

There is no path, only the present moment to live

If God is Love, then God should be a verb, not a noun!

See God in all things

7

The metaphor of darkness as evil is very apt. They are very similar in their physical properties. It is impossible to build a box around darkness and contain it. No walls are thick enough, no structure sturdy enough that can contain darkness. To believe that you could contain darkness or even try means that you do not understand the darkness. The metaphor of love and light is also likewise very appropriate. For just as the smallest amount of light removes darkness wherever it is found, so too the smallest amount of love overcomes fear and evil. Do not try to box in evil. Do not try to insulate yourself or isolate yourself from fear and the evil that others might do. No law, no ritual, no religious incantation can provide the box strong enough to protect us. We can only be protected by the light that removes all darkness. That light is the love that comes from God.

Where is your sanctuary from fearful thoughts? Where do you put your faith and trust? Is it as an addiction? Gambling? Alcohol? Sex? TV? Food? Desiring power? Or is it in the simplicity of love, being non-judgmental and accepting? If your sanctuary is in the physical world then you are searching for that which cannot be obtained. The reason you search is because you fear fear itself. Your thirst will never been quenched. Even if you grasp fear by its horns, twist it, and toss it on the trash heap, it is still exists. Just like the darkness that has been hidden in a box, hidden deep in your heart. It only lies dormant, causing fear that it may one day be awakened. We then begin to fear the fear itself. If, however, your sanctuary deep within your heart is the love that surpasses all human understanding, then there is a light that conquers that darkness. There is peace that reduces all evil to meaningless occurrences, and there is no place that you need to fear. There is no action that should cause concern, for you realize that with love as your sanctuary the world is perfect, you are perfect, God's image is perfect. You become a witness to that perfection, and you find that perfection in all that there is. There is no judgement, for judgement comes from fear. **There is only love**.

We have proof God exists...

Thy faith has made thee whole

Simplicity brings peace of Mind
from this truth you can not hide.
Detaching from the Worldly
and quieting the Mind.

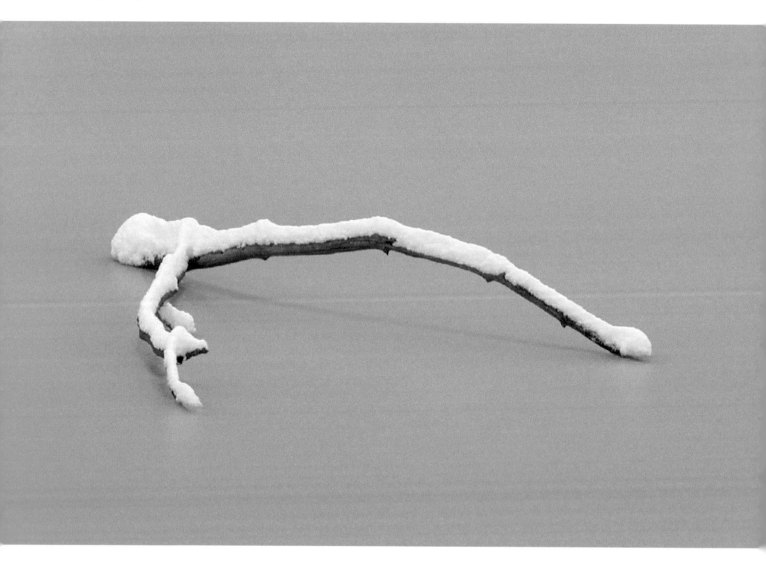

With every breath, we change.
With every thought, we become
a different person.

43

8

If you go into the world this morning angry, you will find the world angry with you. If you go into the world compassionate, looking for Christ in all things, you will find a compassionate world and you will find peace. Early in the morning is when the mind is the most malleable. This is the time when we can shape our day and the outcome of our creative process, the outcome of our world being. How do you start your day? On awakening, take one to two minutes of prayerfulness and compassion to survey your thoughts and to find them all loving and compassionate, filled with gratitude for being able to breathe, for having made it through the night, for being healthy, alive and vibrant in this moment. Ask God to reveal all things to you that need to be revealed. ("Give us this day our daily bread.") Do this for seven days in a row and you will find the world to be more peaceful. You will find your life to be more productive. You will find joy and happiness around every corner.

We have all begun our journey being materialistic, and when we have realized that this path does not work, we abandon our materialism for things spiritual. We grow out of the body into the soul. When one finds the soul to dawn like the morning sun over the vast sea, the clarity of the mind finds no path, only a mysterious universe. We sense that we are a part of that universe, like a wave in the ocean, like a breeze in the wind. We then begin to search for that intelligence beyond our own, a guiding light, a divine spark that blazes within us and all about us to guide us, the spark of love that conquered all darkness, if we only let it shine.

It does not matter what path we take in our search for God, as long as we realize that it is God Himself who is not only the object of our search but also the path. He then becomes the light that fills a room. He becomes the fire that warms the cold night air. How do we find God when we only search for a tiny spark? What then is not God Himself? What things are not a manifestation of His love? Enter your path looking for love, and you will find God. You can't miss Him! There is no more time for speculation or being philosophical. There is only time to enter the path, begin the journey, keeping your life full of grace and love, be pure of heart, and contemplating the world as a manifestation of God. Being mindful of God as love in all things. If we as mortal souls thought of God as much as we think of worldly items, how different our experience would be on the path that He has given us to walk. For through contemplation, purity of heart, we realize that it is no path at all. We do not have to go anywhere, for we are already there. We are surrounded in God's love. All we must do is be.

Silence is just as deadly as radical dogma... No one can speak the mind of God !

Be at peace with God and His creation

9

To "just be" is difficult for most of us, for our being has become clouded with perceptions and misconceptions of what the world is and should be. This is why Jesus said to enter the kingdom, we must do so as little children. We must do so not with dogma, ritual, preconceptions of this or that, or false truths that create fear.

What thoughts lie in the ghetto of your soul? How did they get there? What keeps them there? What feeds them? What kind of rot do they cause in your life? How can you rid your body, how can you rid your mind, how can you rid your soul, how can you rid your being of these thoughts? How can you plant the flowers of love and compassion that change the ghetto of your soul into a vibrant city of Heaven with many mansions? How can you become like that little child you once were?

Your first job is to recognize that such a place exists within you. Your second job is to realize that you nourish it with negativity, and allowing yourself to be guided by fear. Your third job is to realize that you want to remove this blemish. Begin in small steps. It has been said that the way to eat an elephant is one bite at a time. Begin your inner urban renewal project one thought at a time. With every negative thought that creeps into your mind, recognize it for what it is, and then replace it. Try to turn every angry thought into one of compassion. See Christ loving his enemy and remember, what you have done to the least of these you have done to Christ. (Matthew 25:40.) Take one moment at a time. Try not to live in the past. Try not to fear the future. Day by day, step by step, moment by moment you will remove the negative thoughts that poison your mind and being. You will become more fully love and compassion. The more loving and compassionate you become the easier your task. You then rise above the battle field, for you have changed hate and fear into love and compassion. Live the present moment not with judgement based on past perceptions or future fears. When you bring the past into the present, you create a future that does not change, and thus "life" goes on and on and on. *You can only change the present moment, and you can only change it with love*.

If God were a frog, He'd be green… and Heaven would be the pond

Where two or more are gathered...

Everything is a gift from God!

God does not put obstacles on our path that we suffer, but rather that we grow.

10

Let go of life, the life that the ego sees. Live your life, the life that the spirit sees. Find yourself in this moment, for this moment is of the spirit. The ego sees life in the past by what you have, what you had, what you have become, and what you will become. The ego shows this to others and the ego is afraid that all these things will be lost. Whereas, the spirit is sufficient in this moment, and in living this moment we can cast out anger, judgment and live in love, the perfect love that will cast out all fear. Let your prayer be that life is sufficient to serve God and be thankful to God for ALL that he has bestowed upon you. For it is that which has made your spirit find sufficiency in this moment with all the blessings and there in lies the peace.

Living this moment as being sufficient unto itself you are freed from all outcomes. You are freed from judging the outcomes of the ego as being positive or negative, good or bad. There is only perfection as God sees it. "Increase my territory". It is in the present that you realize that your territory always was increased. It was never small to start with, it was only you who had placed it in a box. You set the boundaries. It is in the present, you realize that your thoughts of inadequacy, your thoughts of lack, and your fears are that same box in which you have placed yourself. The power of the Holy Spirit will be the spark whereby, the box is removed so that you can see your territory always was and always will be limited only by the love of God. The illusion of the ego is that there is a box. There is no box, only God's love which is infinite and has no boundaries.

The Mysteries of the Heavens… so affect each other
that a spark in one… ignites a fire in another.
Is the moth drawn to the Light by Love,
or by fleeing from the Fear of Darkness?

Your territory always was and always will be limited only by the love of God.
The moon is not the moon - it is the light of the Sun in darkness.

11

You, therefore, cannot grasp God or love with intellect, but only in the depths of contemplation can you know the secret of his love. For those who do not understand this simple formula, all attempts to explain it will create misconceptions and misinterpretations, half truths that become dogma and ritual that creates obstacles on a path that does not exist. The path implies that we are going somewhere when we are already there. We see heaven apart from ourselves rather than in ourselves. We have changed our vantage point, and although truth still exists, it is elusive because of the illusions created by the intellect rather than a deep knowing of God's love by the contemplative soul. This then is the deepest form of knowledge and wisdom. There is no knowledge and wisdom. That there is no path, only now, only the present moment, only being, not past being or future being, but present being. And in his presence, the creative energy of God manifests. And what is that creative energy? Through contemplation we come to know the secret, and if you have not realized it yet, if it has not been clear, go back and re-read these passages. Find a quiet place to sit and contemplate your relationship with God, how all things have happened to you in your life have brought you to this moment. How all things that will happen in the future depend on this moment—, how this moment is perfect. Nothing can take this moment from you. This moment, in the quietness of your heart, you are connected with God through love. You always have been and always will be through his creative energy, the light of conscious awareness that illuminates the world, God's love.

*Silence can be either imposed, chosen or eternal…all things arise from the eternal silence…
thus silence is the ego's noise…Be silent and know God.*

Negative thoughts destroy us,
of this we can be sure.
So when a thought enters in,
try to make it pure.

Cast out all negativity
and soon you will begin,
To see and feel the
Peace of Christ,
arising from within!!

12

It is our human perception that dictates in this world what is splendid and marvelous, not the saintliness of God's will that provides for each moment. When we suffer, it is our perception that we suffer that causes pain. The egg that is not cracked will never hatch. The body that has never suffered will never grow in spirituality. We see suffering through our bodily eyes as we see the sun in its glory. If we look at obstacles and events with the eyes of our soul, then we see as God sees. We see in the darkness a place of light. We see in ignorance knowledge. We see in pain, growth and in failings, opportunity. Our physical eyes judge guided by our ego. Our spiritual eyes accept, guided by love. We should read the scriptures through the eyes of faith and love, for it would be wrong to read any other way. In the eyes of the spirit each moment is a revelation of God. Each moment is a sacrament. Each moment brings us closer to God's order, God's way, which when our spiritual eyes are opened, we see God in all things. We, therefore, need no faith for we already have our proof. Those who have little faith need works, that they can see with their earthly eyes. Those who have faith, have eyes that will receive the proof but do not need it— for they already see.

Be thankful for each fleeting moment of life...

You are what you are because the world is what it is
Everything that exists does so for a reason
Even you!

61

13

We do not need to be constantly studying and striving to know God's divine action and plan. We only need to become malleable and become part of that plan. When we surrender, we realize that there is a universal spirit that pervades each and every heart, each and every being, and it is planned and it is perfect. This is why Christ said, "What you have done to the least of these, you have done to me". From the great mystery of all there is, there is only One, and we are not separate from God, nor is God separate from us. When we serve each other, we serve God! When we serve God we serve ourselves. (Acts 17:18) In Him we live and move and have our being.

Those who are not satisfied with the divine gifts that are given in the present moment judge themselves to live in the past and do not find contentment. They read books to try and find peace. They dream of peace in the future — if only, or when … then I will find peace. They never surrender themselves to the present but look for peace and spiritual purity in a future time that does not exist. The key is to become aware. Aware of your life in this moment. Aware of God's influence and aware of the influence of the illusion. You cannot become lifted above the battle field until you see the battle. You can not cast out fear with love until you admit that the fear exists and that it is just an illusion. Living in the illusion can cause pain. Living in the illusion allows evil. Until you realize that a demon exists, you cannot say, "In the name of Jesus Christ, demons be gone". It is only in facing the illusion that we can overcome it. When we choose to give it no power over our lives, it evaporates. It is the illusion that separates us from God. When the illusion is evaporated, we realize we were never separate. We had only created a box, placing ourselves in that box. In burying that box in our hearts, we had become dead to the spirit. It is now a time of rebirth, being "born in love" and "of love" rather than "in this world" and "of this world".

In this moment, a moment of longing, by grace alone, we find that peace that passes all understanding. We become the seer and the seen, the knower and the known, the loved and the beloved, and we become Being, not separate from the One who created us but transcendent just as God is transcendent in this material world. We are not light, we are not shadow, we are not fluid, nor solid, but we are a manifestation of the love that has created all the universe. We are what we are. We are unity. We are not I. We are not us. We are Being. In this mystery, you have truly become the sound of one hand clapping. (At this point, you are probably now lost and bewildered by the last statement. Contemplate on this, and when you think you have it figured out, ask. For the answer lies in the beauty of truth and pure love, that can not be experienced by the worldly.) How does a man with no legs give a standing ovation? How does a mute sing praises? How does God speak love with a tree?

Love then becomes the witness, not the works of love, not the works of good, or the avoidance of evil. It is love that is the evidence for our belief in Christ. It is this freedom to love that is rewarded by God. You are free to choose and the choice is not good or evil. The choice is love. Once this choice has been made then all else falls into place. There is no good or evil, just action carried out in perfect love.

Is a moth attracted to the light because of love and desire to be with the light, or is the moth attracted to the light because of fear of darkness and a desire to escape the fear? Do you seek God because of His love and a desire to spend eternity in heaven with God, or do you seek God because of fear to escape the eternity of hell? If you seek God out of love, then you will find heaven on earth, but if you seek God out of fear of eternal hell, then you have found your hell in the present moment.

NOTHING MATTERS BUT LOVE! LOVE IS ALL THERE IS! GOD IS LOVE. ALL ELSE IS JUST AN ILLUSION. THEREFORE, IF LOVE IS ALL THERE IS, AND ALL THAT MATTERS IS LOVE, TO FIND GOD ALL WE NEED TO DO IS LOVE. LET GO OF THE ILLUSION, ALL THAT IS NOT LOVE. WHEN WE FIND CHRIST IN THE LEAST OF THESE, WE FIND LOVE IN THE WORLD. WE ALLOW THE ILLUSION OF IMPERFECTION TO DESEGREGATE AND EVAPORATE. WE SEE ONLY LOVE AND PERFECTION, THAT IS GOD SHINING THROUGH IN ALL THINGS. THAT IS ALL THAT MATTERS. PRAY THAT THE HOLY SPIRIT OPENS YOUR EYES THIS DAY. PRAY THAT THE ANGELS THAT SIT ON YOUR SHOULDER, AND HAVE BEEN WITH YOU CONSTANTLY MAY ACT ON YOUR BEHALF. PRAY THAT YOU MAY SEE WITH THE EYES OF THE SPIRIT AND NOT THE EYES OF THE EGO MIND. PRAY THAT YOU MAY SEE THAT LOVE IS ALL THAT MATTERS AND THAT ALL ELSE IS AN ILLUSION. LIVING THE ILLUSION IS ONLY BRINGING PAIN. LET GO OF THE ILLUSION. SEE THE LOVE. RISE ABOVE THE WORLDLY BATTLES FOR THEY HAVE ALREADY BEEN WON. LOVE IS ALL THAT MATTERS, LOVE IS ALL THAT IS. LOVE IS ALL WE LONG FOR.

Time is an illusion that creates as an illusion that there is no time
For everything there is a season... A time to bloom …

The gifts of God for the people of God, take them in remembrance ...

14

By now, you should realize God may manifest in any form — sometimes an affliction, sometimes an obligation or a duty. God exists in all creatures, and through eyes of the Spirit, one can see the work of divine action in everything. *Every circumstance that exists in the present moment is a gift from God*. If we have the faith that this is a gift, there is nothing that we cannot overcome. We will then learn from our adversity, and we will grow in spirit, and in purpose of our pure heart, being uplifted in faith, finding good in all the gifts, not living in the past or fearing the future. Therefore, we must love our enemies for they, too, are God in action. We must perceive God in the egotism and arrogance of those who seek to do us harm. We must adjust our actions to fit God's purpose, not flinching from adversity but exploring the possibilities and living the adventure of the moment to its fullest. We then will find light in the darkness. The fog will lift, and the sunshine of God's love will shine through. What appeared to be adversity and evil was only a stepping stone toward a better life — a life closer to Christ and unity in the mystical body that unites us all. Surrender to the moment and let God's will be done. Divine action is good and needs no improvement. How can you improve on God's will? You are God's living gospel in the present moment. You are God's flesh made from the word, **today**! That is an awesome responsibility. If you are not aware of God's plan for you, if you are wallowing in the past or wandering aimlessly in the future, then you will miss out on the beauty God intended for you. You shall become insignificant, and your perfection will be hidden. Open up to divine action, for it is pure and simple. Become the Word made manifest to live this moment in awareness that you are the eyes of the world that perceive God in all his glory. Perceive Him, see Him, worship Him, and be thankful this moment has been given to you. All that will remain is to be ready to grasp God who stands beside you and welcome the divine eternity that lasts only in this moment. *Be relieved of the heavy burden of finding God, for He has found you*. (John 14:21)

Is it dawn, or is it dusk?
Is it a new beginning or just "The End"?
As the observer, the choice is yours…

Where are you headed?